51 POEMS

WHAT READERS ARE SAYING ABOUT
51 POEMS

These poems are smart, witty, and lyrically sure of themselves. They build situations rather than tell stories, often in recognizable forms. I enjoyed them.
—Samuel R. Delany, *Dark Reflections*, Dover Books, 2016.

Marcus Bales, in his quiet way, is one of the best poets around. Witty, thoughtful, moving, occasionally painful, these poems are well worth the read, whether you're a poetry fan or not!
—Les Roberts, *The Ashtabula Hat Trick*, Gray and Company Publishers, August 2015.

Marcus Bales has a way of consistently staying light on his feet, even when the subject moves to loved ones lost, missed chances at romance, and the ache of memory. And when the subject is our media-saturated age, puns, poets themselves (and a Lake Erie take on Poe), his wordplay dances gleefully across the page and into the mind.
—Eric Coble, *The Velocity of Autumn*, Dramatists Play Service, 2014

Marcus' poems are clever and cutting, sharp observations on life and love and world events. From ironic commentary on the world, to rueful ruminations on missed connections and lost loves, to mordant observatons of poetry readings, he is the master of deft rhyme and impeccable beat. If you adore form poetry, this is the poetry book of the year: read it!
—Geoffrey Landis

When asked to read these poems, I almost declined. As an English major at Vanderbilt, my approach to poetry, other than such chart-toppers as Kublai Khan and that time Frost took the road less traveled, was a tactical one. "It's simply less print to read than prose," said the fellow student who became the best man in my wedding. To this day, I am suspicious of the crocus, the daffodil and any other plants that led to the Nature effusions of Wordsworth in The Prelude. But Clevelander Marcus Bales has given us plenty from his Muse (Erato was, I believe, the most likely suspect) in this collection. There are both interior and end rhymes, all depicting alienation, reticence, and desolation without being unlikable, shy about the versifying fireworks, or stripped of striking imagery. When a boy, I dreamed of being a tank commander as I gazed at the Sherman tank parked outside a building at the Texas State Fair. In Habu Hill, Bales chooses a shattered tank, climbed over by small boys at an unnamed battlefield long after a war, to depict a palm tree, fed perhaps on the blood of heroes, growing through the top of the open turret as a false sign of rebirth. Then he fiercely denounces the whole idea as just more of the propaganda that's been deluding men and women since before Caesar wrote his Commentaries. These poems both delight and disturb, and what more, besides brevity, can you ask?

—Bill Livingston, *George Steinbrenner's Pipe Dream*, Kent State University Press, 2015

Marcus Bales's *51 Poems* one-ups a Lord Byron quotation about the hyperbolic use of fifty for emphasis. There is a bemused tone to Bales's work, perhaps epitomized by the first poem in the book, a villanelle about the relationship with the reader:

"Of all my readers I like you the best."

Another favorite is "Musing on the Boss Art," a parody of W. H. Auden's "Musee des Beaux-Arts":

"About suffering they were never wrong
The old managers: how well they understood
Its harrowing power; how they took pride
In placing blame directly where it does not belong."

While Bales is also a writer of serious poetry, with strong work on love and war, his true gift is as a witty poet. There he is: fifty plus one.

—Kim Bridgford, *Doll*, Main Street Rag Publishing Co., 2014.

An impressive 51 poems, all poised and formal in their control, but varied in their approach and subject matter. Paying homage to the skill of old masters like Byron, Poe, Keats, Shakespeare and W.S. Gilbert, parts of the collection rage across the modern world as though Dryden had come back and gleefully realized how much more there is to attack than in his day. Bales does satire in the grand manner and skewers his targets: general idiocy, political stupidity, bad faith, bad politics, free verse, bad poetry readers, and modern literary theory in memorable images and lines. Like the best of satire revelation creeps out from behind the banter and gives the reader a good swift kick.

The poems are entertaining, enjoyable to read, and multilayered. As Bales writes in "Accomplishment":

> What I want is that smile from those who know
> The difficulties speed and grace have hidden

While all the poems stand alone, part of the fun of reading some of them lies not just in recognizing what some poems are modeled on, but the way the new poem plays with, or sometimes against, the original.

Marcus Bales has the gift of making the language of form sound natural and the events of everyday life seem extraordinary."

— Gail White, *Asperity Street*, Able Muse Press, 2015

I recall one time reading an anthology of "modern"American poets, and in among the impenetrable, incomprehensible, unreadable stuff was a "poem" that consisted of a single word on the page. One word. On the page. A "poem." By a "modern" American poet. And I was done. Finished! I couldn't read another word, another page of this "anthology." It was impossible.

Well, these days I've been reading *51 Poems* by Marcus Bales. And what a joy! The poems come alive and tumble from the page and through the senses like liquid, smooth and warm. It's true. It's hard to imagine how easy on the senses a book of so-called "form" can be. But it is! It is poignant and funny and brilliantly crafted. Here, for example, is the Marcus Bales take on Gandhi—

> This supercallusedfragilemystic
> hexedbyhalitosis.

51 Poems is easy to read. Incredibly easy. And that is quite a feat for a poet whose proficiency with form seems to come as easily as water from a faucet. Whether Marcus is channeling Robert Frost, as in the tender "Stopping by the Phone on a Silent Evening" ...

> I listen to her disavow
> in silence silence, yet, somehow
> still ask if I am sorry now,
> still ask if I am sorry now.

... or writing about a car ride,

>   sitting between my angry mother
>   and my father's driving thigh.

Marcus delivers powerfully and warmly, and with honor to the craft of poetry, its artistry:

>   And everything I felt was blurred
>   by those metallic whines I heard
>   whenever we pulled out to pass
>   the slower cars
>   whose lower notes were clear
>   below the shift down into passing gear.

In this world of poems where impenetrability, unintelligibility, and surfaces like granite seem to garner all the attention, here is *51 Poems*. A must read. It is a balm in poetry land.

>   —John L. Stanizzi, *Dance Against the Wall, Hallelujah Time!* and
>   other titles.

Marcus Bales applies the steel of form to an assortment of materials: old memories, new news, undying passions, eternal poems, and ephemeral po-biz. The result is always a high polish, often a cutting edge, and sometimes a skewer.

>   —Maryann Corbett, *Mid Evil*, University of Evansville Press,
>   2015.

In *51 Poems*, Marcus Bales reveals a rare talent. Some of the included poems are charming, others are touching, some are comedic, and many contain unusual imagery that is utterly original yet easily understandable. Various emotional threads flow through the writings, and a bittersweet sense of loss and missed opportunities underlie many of the more powerful verses. But perhaps the most remarkable aspect to this collection is that whether one of Bales's poems is tragic, amusing, or simply descriptive, its meaning is consistently crystal clear. I suggest you read it, and enjoy.

>   —Rajnar Vajra, author of "Her Scales Shine Like Music"
>   appearing at Tor.com August 2016, and "Progress Report"
>   appearing in Analog SF and Fiction around April, 2016.

With the same deftness that evokes bittersweet memories of childhood, Marcus Bales can convince you to exonerate him from doing-in a poet who goes on a poem or two (or three) too long at a reading. But fear not, Marcus does not go on too long in this collection of wise and witty poems. You are not likely to forget these final lines from "Have You Forgotten":

> The wine, the bread, that sad, sad tune
> and me?

Or these (I'll leave you to find the poem)

> I'm dancing at a cliff edge, unaware
> Of where the precipice gives way to air.

And while you are looking for that poem, don't be surprised to come across

> supercallousedfragilemystic
> hexedbyhalitosis.

How will the poet rhyme it? It might be absurder than his rhyme for murder. Dig in!
—Edmund Conti, *Eddies*, Runaway Spoon Press, 1994.

Those already familiar with Bales' facility and wit will enjoy this collection, which is filled to the brim with his signature erudite, deeply humane humor. Those who aren't familiar with him should be. Whether he's aiming his carefully drawn bons mots at bad poetry, or bad philosophy, or bad priests and politicians, I'm with him. And when he's showing he knows himself to be a fool, I'm a fool right there with him.
—Mark Vian, *StreamTracking,* Purple Mountain Press
Forthcoming September 2016

51 Poems takes us back to a time when literary poetry was more popular and popular poetry was more literary. Light but not frivolous, serious but not dour, and combining "how does he do it" technical virtuosity with deep feeling, these poems are a tremendous pleasure to read. A great book to give to people who think they don't like poetry (i.e. almost anyone).
—Pino Coluccio

Marcus Bales' skill is not just in the craft of meter and rhyme, though this is apparent in virtually everything he writes and reminds you of Nash and contemporary poets like Britain's Nigel Forde. He also has a knack of getting at his subjects from odd angles, so you come to them afresh, following in on the poet's own trajectory. So, we don't see much peace in the world, because it's out drinking with Becket's Godot; a leaving, possibly the end of a romance, is likened to the start of an Amelia Earhart-style flight and a well-conceived sestina has the poet chasing his own tail while trying to get to wash the car. *51 Poems* covers a wide variety of subjects in a fresh, original way, without ever leaving the comfort of well-loved forms and rhythms.

—Simon Williams, *A Place Where Odd Animals Stand*,
Oversteps Books, 2012

In these days of modish, often impenetrable, utterance passed off as poetry, Marcus Bales is a most welcome voice, always rhyming but never with strain or the slightest contrivance, and touching the heart, be it with pathos, satire, reminiscence. His is a formidable talent. His masters might be Belloc, Chesterton, or de la Mare in his more whimsical moods, but Bales is always genuine, and himself. This is, quite simply, a splendid book.

—Roger Craik, *Down Stranger Roads*, BlazeVox, 2014

Marcus Bales' collection, *51 Poems*, is finely welded into a whole. Like good sculpture, he works within the ebb and flow of the page, pulling seeming unrelated parts into a coherent whole. And like good sculpture, there are times you can see the beads where the parts were welded together. One of the features of our contemporary poetry is that many poets run away from poetics. Not Bales. Courageous and intelligent, he takes advantage of all the words have to offer—with a sly wink to boot.

—Stephen Dowdall, *Paradise Texas On the Rocks*, LP, 2005

51POEMS

MARCUS BALES

For Linda

CVIII

When people say, "I've told you *fifty* times,"
They mean to scold, and very often do;
When poets say, "I've written *fifty* rhymes,"
They make you dread that they'll recite them too;

—*Lord Byron*

Contents

I Like You The Best

Of all my readers I like you the best.
You're sexily well-read, and very smart—
oh, you're the one; the rest are just the rest.

Though most of them will think I speak in jest,
it's you, you know, who's read into my heart:
of all my readers I like you the best.

I'm feeling better now that I've confessed
that it's for you I struggle with my art.
Oh, you're the one—the rest are just the rest.

I see by your reaction you had guessed
I liked you more, and liked you from the start;
of all my readers, I like you the best.

You get me—and I like how you're impressed
that I know Horace comes before Descartes;
ah, you're the one. The rest are just the rest.

I like you very much—I'd be distressed
at anything that kept us two apart.
Of all my readers I like you the best;
Oh, you're the one: the rest are just the rest.

ACCOMPLISHMENT

Every rail was different: some were rotted
and simply broke leaving, after a fall,
a long step down; some so thoroughly knotted
I wondered how they held together at all.
Some weren't seated in their posts and slipped
or turned to throw me off, and some so bent
or warped I wondered how they'd even ripped
a rail from such a tree. And so it went:
I fell a lot until I finally knew
the balance tricks I needed where and when.
I got to know each twist and warp and skew
by falling off and getting up again.

And then one day I walked it all the way
straight down that zigzag fence without a fall.
And then I tried for grace, backwoods ballet,
then speed, and then I nearly ruined it all:
I took my mother to show what I could do.
And all the charms that speed and grace confer,
my whole accomplishment, all that I knew,
was only dangerous fooling around to her.
So she declared the fence was out of bounds—
which didn't stop me walking it, of course—
permission or officially sanctioned grounds
for action hasn't ever been the source
of what I've done or what still makes me go.
What I want is that smile from those who know
the difficulties speed and grace have hidden
no matter how forbidding or forbidden.

Habu Hill

We called it Habu Hill. The men who'd dug
and died and crawled and killed about where we
played army must have named it by its height.
The MPs caught me one day, trying to lug
a box of antitank shells home with me;
the box's lid had rusted on too tight
for me to take just one. Their tires screamed,
and even I could tell the men were scared
of what I had. I wondered that I'd dared
a thing so much more dangerous than it seemed.

They made me show them where I'd found the box.
They took the rotted uniforms, the gun;
they labeled and took each whole and shattered bone,
then blocked the entrance of the cave with rocks
we couldn't possibly move, and spoiled our fun.
We didn't show them the tank, overgrown
and buried, about fifty yards away
and down the hill. So we just moved our game
of army over there, and played the same
old roles of death that soldiers' children play.

I used to dare to think the hole down through
the bottom of that dead American tank
between the ruined treads must once have fed
on special blood, because a palm tree grew
up through that hole, up through the ravaged, dank
insides, up through the hatch, as if the dead,
by standing back up through their war machine
in such a form won back the lives they'd lost
at war, and brought some peace that war had cost,
and stood for what they'd died to make life mean.

I used to dare to think that. Now I know
it for the hopeful bullshit that it was,
denial yoked to ignorance by dread.
I've heard the stories grinding to their slow
halts of bunched fists and clenched jaws
as no one said the things that can't be said,
that there is nothing good, or just, or true,
or beautiful, or in proportion, and death
distorts and fear corrupts from breath to breath
everything we hope that we can do.

What VD Taught Me

They did it every year for years
and every year I grew more wary
and up to puberty my fears
were focused on mid-February.

The cards were always white and red
except their most essential feature
was number, and I came to dread
that single envelope from teacher.

One single envelope can yet
bring dread with undiminished force.
I leave it, waiting 'til I get
some more—except for checks, of course.

SCARY HOME-LIFE

for GTZ

Get up, get out, and get away—I went
as early as I could to leave one vile
exposure for another. School. It meant
escape from home at least a little while,
not long enough, and trading family guile
for reading sullen peers and teacher spin,
except for you, beside me on the aisle—
I was the girl with the scary home-life and bad skin.

I was first to homeroom every day.
And how did Mr Romo ever know
that half a sausage sandwich was the way
a skinny girl survived. He'd always go
"Good morning," handing me a half as though
that half were mine and we were somehow kin;
I'd nod my thanks and sit in the back row—
I was the girl with the scary home-life, and bad skin.

And you, who sat beside me, always kind
to me, and always kind of sassy tough
to other kids who other years combined
to make me almost miserable enough
to stay at home, from you I learned to bluff
my inner fear, to fake a cocky grin,
and start to walk as if it wasn't rough
to be the girl with the scary home-life, and bad skin.

L'envoi
Yeah, it was you and Mr Romo, in the end,
who gave me things that I could not begin
to pay you back for, so even I'd befriend
the girl with the scary home-life, and bad skin.

BACK ON THE TOUR

An architectural tour was how we met.
We ooh-ed and ah-ed and craned our necks to see.
But I got all the beauty I could get
by watching her pretend to not watch me.

The tour had left us in the theater.
We walked out on the empty stage and stood.
Our breathing seemed to echo through the hall.
She grinned at me, and I grinned back at her.
She sang a phrase, and heavens! she was good.
I did less well, but still, not bad at all.
She sang her favorite songs, and I sang mine,
until we found a love song we both knew.
We started off and we were doing fine
until we got about three-quarters through
and realized at the end the actors kissed.

We stood there, just a step too far apart
and when we should have stepped together stepped
away, and faltered over words we'd missed,
and stopped. And then it seemed too late to start
again with just the little bit we'd kept.
And so we walked off stage, and went to find
the group we'd worked so hard to get behind.
We ooh'ed and ah'ed again, back on the tour,
only sure we'd never quite be sure.

Warm and Dry

There wasn't any moon. The gathering mist
had drifted toward the fog that coiled and fanned
in slowly, nearer and nearer, from the lake.
And there we stood, each waiting to be kissed.
We knew it wouldn't take the promised land,
nor ripe, forbidden fruit, to make us make
the final move. The fog moved in and met
the mist and merged; the tide below surged in.

We listened to it sucking at the shore
we couldn't see as we were wrapped with wet,
caressing chills. How warm and dry her skin
felt when I brushed her arm with mine—and for
a pulse the night seemed bright, the air all clear,
the tide its urgent highest for us to ride.

But we had each been taken before, and eyed
each other sideways, both of us afraid
that any move we made would break the poise
we'd barely held 'til then. So there we stayed,
not touching, while the fog and dark and noise
re-tempted us. And then we said goodbye,
each still alone, and neither warm nor dry.

STOPPING BY A PHONE
ON A SILENT EVENING

for Norman Ball

Whose call this is I think I know—
she's staying with her mother, though.
She calls in silence like a swan
across the city, through the snow.

She hates to waste her silence on
an empty room so when she's gone
she calls to let me hear her say
the naught from which she won't be drawn.

The only sound I hear's the grey
and empty hollowness of stray
electrons that the lines endow
with hiss that softly leaks away.

I listen to her disavow
in silence silence, yet, somehow
still ask if I am sorry now,
still ask if I am sorry now.

INTERSTATE

Hear it? Hear the way that buzz has slurred
our voices down to monotone?
It's still the same unnerving sound
I heard when I would ride
between my angry mother
and my father's driving thigh
and watch, through first one half-closed eye
and then the other,
the blazing road lights glaring by.
I used to hum the tires' empty wail
along the short chromatic scale,
up and down, and up and down again,
I droned within its narrow range of tone,
A beat behind in groaned cacophony.

All I used to see
was what the windshield's tinted glass,
the dashboard lights, and the distant stars
could soften for me, even hide.
And everything I felt was blurred
by those metallic whines I heard
whenever we pulled out to pass
the slower cars
whose lower notes were clear
below the shift down into passing gear.

And now it's ours whose vowels are drowned
beneath that numbing moan;
now I am at the wheel, instead
of playing safe at sleep as I did then.
So let's not fight again.
Hinted at by all those brake-lights wound
up in this interstate ahead,
out of sight and up a grade,
our exit waits. And I'm afraid.
I'm afraid, I said.
Afraid in all our going on
that all that's changed is how we've gone
from ancient doubt to new uncertainty;
afraid that all there is is what we hear
no further back no matter where we steer.

Pre-Flight

A tired, blood-shot moon was staring down
half-closed with puffy clouds, as if the night
before had been too hard, too late, too much.
The wind was building like a headache, brown
around its sharpening edges. It blurred my sight,
and grit was all that I could taste or touch.

She ran her engine up and down to test,
then shut it off, climbed out, and zipped her vest
against the wind. She paid her bill in cash
and turned at last to me. And there we were.
I tried to say how much I wished she'd change
her mind, in spite of everything, and stay.
We talked about the wind, her fuel and range,
and where she'd land, and how long she should rest.
I'd nearly nerved myself to reach for her
and try to say it somehow anyway
when over to the east a pinkish flash
went off like an alarm to send her west.

We'd waited there together for the dawn
and it had come too soon. The sky was clear
the moon had set, the wind was just a breeze.
could lifetimes really turn on things like these?
I called good-bye. By then she couldn't hear.
I pulled the chocks away, and she was gone.

BROKEN SUNLIGHT

"Something isn't right," she finally said,
"But I can't tell you what I think is wrong."
His posture showed he hadn't understood,
But he was not the sort to lose his head—
And if he were, he'd waited way too long.
She left as if she meant to leave for good.

So there, amid the kitchen's early gloom,
He breakfasts on espresso for his nerves
And watches, while the beveled glass appears
To break the sunlight glittering through the room,
The icy drops on awnings' scalloped curves
That grow until they droop like fattened tears.

Hunched, crossed arms on uncrossed knees,
He thinks about those liquid points of light
That hang as if it's they who need to think—
How, slowly bulged with brightness, each one frees
Itself in tiny flashing bursts of white
That prism through the glass and make him blink.

And, blinking at those droplets' rainbowed streaks
That leave, as she left, neither note nor trace
Besides a little flash in a brightening sky,
He sits with tear-shaped shadows on his cheeks
And broken sunlight streaming down his face
And still, with all that help, he does not cry.

HAVE YOU FORGOTTEN

Have you forgotten the dark piano bar,
the cloud-dimmed dusk, the steady drip of rain,
and, later, clothing scattered near and far,
the warming, clearing skies, the morning star,
        champagne?

Have you forgotten Niagara's rumbling roar,
the crack of calving ice in Hubbard Bay,
the gaudy light's long Key West sunset shore,
the one last day in Paris just before
        it's May?

Have you forgotten it all, and all so soon;
don't you recall the phosphorescent sea,
the beach, the stars, the driftwood fire, the moon,
the wine, the bread, the cheese, that sad, sad tune,
        and me?

ME AND THE MOON

For Alex Bevan

Her presence was the organizing spice
that made the dish; the multivalent pun;
the compliment whose humor takes you twice
as far aback in unexpected fun,
her laughter tinkling like a scoop of ice
cubes thrown on glass bottles in the sun
that heats a summer vacation afternoon.
This morning though it's only me and the moon.

Me and the distant moon, who's not as far
away as she and I have now become.
She laughs that laugh while I sit in this bar
and wonder how I could have been so dumb
to leave where all the things I value are
and vanish in this alcoholic slum,
regretting what I've kept and what I've strewn
this morning when it's only me and the moon.

And now the moon is pretty far advanced
along its ambit's arc above this place
where one is propositioned, not romanced,
and conversation lacks both wit and grace.
I shuffle now where once I might have danced
and face the fact that this is what I face,
however jaded or inopportune,
this morning while it's only me and the moon.

L'envoi
Barman! Bring another tinkling glass
or two, and we will claim that we're immune
to all this pitiful alas alas
this morning, you, and me, and the goddamned moon.

DANCING WITH ABANDON

The children squeal and clap and call,
      Dancing with abandon;
Their laughter doesn't pause or pall—
They step and leap without a fall
And never seem to sweat at all,
      Dancing with abandon.

Their costumes swirl in scented air,
      Dancing with abandon;
They smile and sing without a care
With curls and ribbons in their hair
As if some magic kept them there
      Dancing with abandon.

I'd like to spin across that floor,
      Dancing with abandon—
I've done it many times before,
But now I'm old, and guard the door,
And think too much, and go no more
      Dancing with abandon.

PRECIPICE

Intent on someone else's words, your lips
not quite a smile that hints at quips the sass
of one raised eyebrow shows, your fingertips
arranged around a long-bulbed shape of glass,
you glance at me with richly chocolate eyes,
between a tilt of head and brush of hand
to flip a strand of hair, and improvise
a flickered wink that strips me where I stand.
You leave me shivering, trying not to stare,
remembering times you're unconfined by those
expensive clothes, while quivering to compose
my face, and knowing everybody knows
I'm dancing at a cliff edge, unaware
of where the precipice gives way to air.

Dark Fails

A sure surge of self seems
        to stop—hover
in strong, strange, occult gleams—
        and glow above her;

I feel force like a huge old
        magic treasure
suffused in gathered gold
        take my small measure.

It's here—here where dark fails
        and light thickens
with this woman that life sails
        and love quickens.

TRACKS

The freezer hums its lowest notes
        the refrigerator too;
the furnace rumbles, hot air floats
        in over covers askew.

A failing neon bulb descants
        above the feral cats'
busy tenors, thumps, and pants,
        blinking 'Parts' then 'Pats'.

My keyboard's intermittent ticks,
        intimately slight,
add their small percussive licks
        in rhythm with the night.

It only needs a bluesy love
        song on a saxophone
to blend in with the memories of
        last night's delicious moan.

Besottedly I hum and blow
        and buzz and wah and coo
through every love song that I know
        in love, in love, with you.

Quantum Mechanics

for Ralph Oman

We squint in spray, barely keeping our eyes
open—the things we see we have to fight
to see, blinking through the stinging salt
and aching sun against the looming size
of wind-snapped crests. The brutal sun's so bright
that every trough could be a moving fault
and every heaving wave a flaw the vale
of space and time does not define. I trim
the sail, but through the spray and sun it's him
I watch. He sails as if he couldn't fail
to do whatever he sets out to do,
as if his will alone could steer us through
and change each one of these anomalies
of wind and wave to navigable seas.

RACQUETBALL

He smiles with quick excitement, creasing balls
with hard short strokes no matter what the score
and leaves opponents nothing left to play.
He crushes winners hard against the walls
or kills them in the corners at the floor
while others die untouched to roll away.
He doesn't like to win, he likes to beat
his victims, beat them down until they feel
they're beaten, beat them till they never heal,
till when they see him they still feel defeat.

What's he lost that hooked its barbed demand
to be regained so deep? And though he's not
unfriendly in the focused way he's got
to prove he's good, I still don't understand
why everybody else has got to lose
before he finds a triumph he can use.

MEETING SMITH

I don't remember just precisely when
or where we met, or who that we were with,
but I remember heat and pool, and then
a fight with several large anonymous men.
And as you clubbed the last one with your cue
I said "Nice shot." And you growled, "Yeah. You, too."
              Remember Smith?

Another time some newbie uniforms
were hitting on some women we were with—
you warned them they were pushing at the norms
of civilized behavior—oh, it warms
the heart to think of how polite you are
before we clear out an entire bar,
              Chevalier Smith!

And though we are not now the men we were,
among these soft civilians we are with
I've seen your fuse get lit and heard that "Grrr"
that warned me: find a stick because the fur
is just about to fly. But now we're older
And Lady puts her hand upon your shoulder
              And calms you, Smith.

But someday we'll be in some drinking spot
and some guys that we're having trouble with
will show us quite abruptly that we're not
the hardest guys around, and what we've got
of all that we've got left is not enough,
and time and youths will teach we're not so tough—
              But not yet, Smith.

OLD FIGHTER PILOT

He's an old fighter pilot,
and he lived a life hotter than most,
though you can't tell by looking
and he'd be the last one to boast—
unless he's been drinking,
and he hasn't been sober in days;
but standing there so
drunk that two each of everything sways
he'll bet you and beat you
at your game or his, loser pays.

He's an old fighter pilot,
and he lived a life hotter than most,
though he seems sort of harmless there
staring like he's seen a ghost—
cause mostly he has,
and the ghosts that he sees are his friends,
some of them better than him,
and their too-early ends;
and he sees their heroics more clearly
through a single malt lens.

He's an old fighter pilot,
and he lived a life hotter than most—
when he thinks of the women, he smiles,
and mutters a toast,
reviewing the range and array
of shape, color, and size—
though each of them second
to aircraft whose memories he flies—
and he jacks a quick double
to cough, and then wipe at his eyes.

He's an old fighter pilot,
and he lived a life hotter than most,
though you can see clearly
he's stretching a glide toward the coast:
he's zeroing distance
and auguring in through a haze;
but standing there so
drunk that two each of everything sways
he'll still bet and beat you
at your game or his—loser pays.

This Bar

In the middle of their movie each arrives
smiling in this gutter, still the stars
of broad moments in their narrow lives.
They tell of other people, other bars,
other husbands, lovers, friends, and wives,
re-writing both their pleasures and their scars;
how one thing given up another strives
to get; how what one shines another tars
with one of the varieties of hate.
But here the villain is a dead-end job
or marriage, or failing kids; it would be great
if Yankees, Nazis, drug lords, or The Blob
were why we're lost, or losing, or alone—
but here the tales and failures are our own.

UBI SUNT

for Mark Vian

Ubi sunt the Romans used to write
whenever it came near the time of year
for bare ruined choirs and dying light
shadowed across the chilly lack of cheer.
I guess it isn't much above the odds:
as dark approaches people check their bets,
and even grope a little after gods,
as surely as the daylight time sun sets.

There are a few I wonder where they are—
not gods but people—when something seen or said
has cracked a shadowed memory door ajar—
as you smile now, or maybe nod your head,
because you've just remembered one or two
whose lives have lapsed to distant silhouettes
who once were close as anyone to you,
as surely as the daylight time sun sets.

Where are they now?—it's been that long?—and why
did such a close connection fray away?
But we lead busy lives, and with a sigh
for lang syne not unshadowed by dismay,
turn back to those who love us here and now,
and whom we love, in spite of our regrets
for absent others time does not allow
as surely as the daylight time sun sets.

L'envoi
You! *Hypocrite semblable!* Spare
me all your can't recalls and I forgets!
We each remember all that we can bear
as surely as the daylight time sun sets.

FLATTERY

You flatter, to begin with, well-rehearsed,
and subtle as the assonantal vowel;
but though you might start quietly at first
you quickly lay it thickly with a trowel.
Oh, everybody does it—don't be shy.
Although it is a self-effacing craft
just give a little flattery a try
and maybe get ahead and not the shaft.
Amusingly, they never do catch on—
the brass thinks they deserve to be the brass—
that compliments from underlings are drawn
from bowels of bullshit pulled out of your ass.
Flatter then; it serves its social function
If you remember smarm follows unction.

DRINKING WITH GODOT

Peace will not arrive again, today.
Each reflex action paws the ground and roars,
and you don't hear the things I have to say
and I don't listen well enough to yours.
Peace will not arrive again, this year.
No recent book, nor one from long ago,
Will teach us how to live without our fear
while peace is still out drinking with Godot.

It's hard to wait the time that peace can take
to work things out so justice, beauty, truth,
and some sense of proportion overtake
the violent impatiences of youth.
War is irreducibly insane;
if I know anything, that's what I know.
And if we fight instead of we explain
then peace will stay out drinking with Godot.

We don't get peace because there's not a war—
or not a big one, or not one very close.
Peace is choosing: choosing to explore
alternatives before you diagnose
a circumstance as needing violent means;
peace is not a lack, it's status quo
we ruin when we send in the marines—
and also send peace drinking with Godot.

L'envoi:
All of us—we're all in part to blame
for finding tantrums easier to throw
than finding out how much we're all the same
and want peace back from drinking with Godot.

GRINNING HENCHMEN

They do not wake up sharing bwahahas
with grinning henchmen as they shave, and think
"Today I shall be evil!" No, the laws
are on their side. They never even blink
at all the tears and suffering they cause.
They've got their lives to live, and they don't shrink
from living them, like you and me, with flaws
and virtues, growing families, food and drink,
and love and death. They look at life and view it
just like us. But in our common murk
they did each evil deed and never knew it
to be evil. No one, king to clerk,
has thought they're doing evil as they do it—
they always think they're doing some god's work.

How Can We Learn

At any given time on earth
there are about three dozen wars
where older people think it's worth
their children's lives to settle scores.

It never is. You cannot teach
your neighbor not to hit you back
by being first or fast to breach
the peace with physical attack.

But money calls, the arms increase,
we do what common sense forbids;
how can we learn to live in peace
by killing one another's kids?

Nothing Saved

I guess I was about sixteen
when TIME killed God and filled the scene
with rock 'n' roll and an empty culture of sales.
They sold their copies, sold their ads,
and touted all the modern fads
while everybody chased their holy grails.

We grew up soft and grew up slow
with too much sex and dope and dough
and a sense the world was ours and we were cool.
We sassed the teachers we didn't like
and then if punished called a strike,
demanding relevance or we'd close the school.

Our parents, who had fought the War,
refused to fight with us, and swore
we'd have the best of all they had to give.
So coddled carefully by cash
we spent our school years talking trash
instead of learning how we ought to live.

Now you sell that and I sell this,
your style of shit, my brand of piss,
each shuck and shuffle prompts a jive and dodge.
We lease the things that we can't buy
and then we can't remember why
we've got that junk piled up in our garage.

We hate the boss, dislike our teachers,
fear the friends who're over-reachers,
and up is how we always think we're wised.
We want promotion or a raise,
so, pusillanimously, praise
in public people privately despised.

We think our social credit's good
and we have always thought we would
get comped to cruise among those Golden Isles
where everyone is thin and young,
and well-endowed and better-hung,
and we go free on Frequent Flyer miles.

We claim our lives are good and clean—
by which we almost always mean
we don't get caught, and laugh ironic laughter;
we just expect to get away
with everything we do or say
while deferential others clean up after.

But deference demands respect,
and we had little to collect,
and what we had is very nearly spent:
spent in drinks and puffs and snorts,
spent on sex and other sports,
spent without a clue to what it meant.

And now at last we're growing old
we carp about it getting cold
without the warm resilience of our youth.
For we have nothing saved or earned—
the pleasure domes to which we turned
are too well-tuned to ever tell the truth:

There's nothing left except the husks
of what we could have been, and dusks
of punishing regret we've yet to sample.
Save the world? We didn't try.
We used it up, and can't deny
our legacy will be our bad example.

GIVING UP FOR LENT

On the resignation of Pope Benedict XVI

The serious ascetics set the bar
And starve themselves for forty nights and days;
The rest of us are just the way we are
And give up meat, merlot, or mayonnaise,
Convinced that that will get us just as far
And earn the same amount of holy praise.
I know how good I feel when I repent,
And give up giving up for Lent for Lent.

The Pope, though, went too far: he's left us floored.
This year for Lent he gave up being Pope.
What kind of leadership is that, and Lord!—
If we all quit our jobs to pray and hope,
Then where will nuns and priests get room and board
On tithes of nothing—is he smoking dope?
And who'll protect a hierarchy infested
With pedophiles, and keep them unarrested?

The mind, though it may not exactly boggle,
Can not remain unboggled at the thought
That Putin-like behind the scenes he'll toggle
The levers of a Cardinal that he's got
In mind to be Medvedev—a boondoggle
To keep in place regressions he has sought
Embracing Paulist not the Christian ways:
No independent thought, no girls, no gays.

I can't imagine something more injurious
Than failing social good and liberation
In favor of repression like the curia's,
Which promises the poor that their salvation
Will come through work and widows' mites—I'm furious
At all the money spent on decoration
Instead of education and clean water
By men who'll fuck your son and whore your daughter.

They clog us up like mucus in a lung,
Immune to all except the penicillin
Of revolution's billion-throated tongue;
But we are what we are, and we're unwilling
To do what saints have done or mockers sung.
And so he sits there, smiling like a villain,
And has the cake that he is eating, too.
And who will pay in cash and freedom? You.

The World Remakes Itself

The world remakes itself until it's strange
to us, and then again, until the state
of being strange itself has been undone
by being strange. And when the news gets back
to us about what happened it's always late,
and actions that we finally had begun
are overtaken by events, or fate.
From Marathon to Athens at the run
to real-time Youtube combat from Iraq,
the context of each battle lost or won
is viewed through faulty lenses fogged or black
with myth, illusion, zealotry, or hate.
However fast or slow the news may range
the speed of understanding doesn't change.

BLACK HILLS

The ancients in their ancient lands once carved
their leaders' faces in their native stone.
But here the natives, shot, betrayed, and starved,
were forced to leave their holy hills alone.
Now, having stamped the people out, we stamp
our heroes' faces on this sacred rock,
and build a parking lot where RVs camp,
and children screech, and smug white tourists gawk.
We can't see the offense. But we'd have seen
if, when the Muslims held Jerusalem
they'd built a tourist center by that green
hill far away, and made a shrine for them
to show the righteousness of their hegemony
by carving Caliphs' heads above Gethsemane.

RULE NUMBER ONE

For Linda, who said it first

If you're going to have a reading
    then no matter where you are
for a minimum of breeding
    you have got to have a bar.

You will fill up all your seating,
    they will come from near and far,
if the best part of your greeting
    is "Why, yes we have a bar!"

But the evening will be fleeting
    even if you've booked a star
when it's alcohol they're needing
    and you do not have a bar.

They will freeze in scanty heating
    and they'll swelter till they char
if you advertise by leading
    with the fact you have a bar.

Though it's raining or it's sleeting
    if you offer them a jar
they'll be aleing, beering, meading,
    and absinthing at the bar.

But when poetry starts bleeding
    out of every scab and scar
all you'll see is me retreating
    if you haven't got a bar.

Poetry Reading

Her voice a buzzing monotone,
          she first intoned her title,
her mouth too near the microphone
she said, I think, our souls would moan
with howls like Allen Ginsberg's own,
and slurred and blurred her dreary drone
          in tedious recital.

She gripped the lectern on the stage,
          her poem never ending—
and only her decrepit age
assuaged the next three readers' rage
as, turning yet another page,
she spent our time as if her wage
          depended on its spending.

As moderator, I did not
          perceive a lot of choice
as murmurs grew: somebody ought,
no, had, to halt her verbal squat
so toad-like in our garden spot,
and find a way to staunch this rot
          by stoppering her voice.

So arms out toward, as I'd been taught,
          the middle of the mass,
I aimed, breathed out, and squeezed, and shot
the leather-lunged and doddering blot
who'd droned along as if she thought
that once she'd seized the mike she'd got
          some sort of life-time pass.

The general approach of Law,
       and many of its minions,
to shooting someone through the craw
for her inane blah blah blah blah,
however last that last last straw,
is that it is a fatal flaw
       in not a few opinions.

The prosecutor even shed
       a manly tear to show it
had moved him greatly she was dead:
"Her pure poetic spirit fled
prosaic Death's pedestrian tread . . ."
"Wait, wait—" the jury foreman said.
       "You say she was a poet?"

The prosecutor said "Indeed!
       and she was published widely.
I'll use your question to proceed
to show you." He began to read.
At length, the foreman knelt to plead:
"Stop reading! We have all agreed!
       we can't abide this idly!

"You've put us through this punishment
       and made your case absurder;
we find the shooter innocent
of any criminal intent—
indeed, we actively lament
your silly try to represent
       this noble act as murder.

"We hold free speech must know its place
          if it is to continue:
you must not underbid your ace,
nor doubt the Holy Spirit's grace,
nor sing the tune if you're a bass,
for decency demands you face
          the moral law within you!

"But poets who have read too long
          must all be superseded.
We urge you when you're in a throng
while poets thus are in the wrong,
to make your protest very strong
and aim to end such ceaseless song
          with shot and shell as he did!"

The prosecutor gave a sigh
          and packed away his pleadings,
then gave me such a look goodbye
it made me think he meant to try
to mutely say, or just imply,
that maybe I'd be wise if I
          no longer read at readings.

POET BIOS

Some are longer than the poem; some are sly
or arch, but most are dry
recitations
of lists of publications
or hobbies or pets,
Frequently a wife or husband gets
a mention, or the occasional contest win,
or a selection in
a "Best Of" collection,
a Mensa or Phi Beta Kappa connection,
or maybe a prize
or two, or nominations or other such tries,
and sometimes fellowships or kids,
but some common concordance forbids
any sort of real
revelation. Yet, there's an awkward feel
from almost every one
that quite a bit more work was done
on the bio than on the poem.
By their bios shall you know 'em.

NOTGETTINGITITUDINOSITY

For John Bales, who coined the word

At first I thought perhaps it could be me
who'd missed why he was hostile and confused—
but one by one the whole group seemed to be
persuaded by his comments that he oozed
some notgettingititudinosity.

It's not like he was told to take a knee,
or anyone demanded to be schmoozed;
it's more he seemed determined he would pee
in everybody's Wheaties—none refused
in notgettingititudinosity.

He hadn't given us a clue why he
was angry when the rest were just amused,
nor why he seemed to think that he was free
to demonstrate so clearly unexcused
notgettingititudinosity.

If unpursued the guilty still will flee
perhaps it's likewise true that the abused
attack potential friends whom they don't see
as friendly, since they're blinded by a bruised
notgettingititudinosity.

It hurts each time some new-encountered "we"
rejects a person when he thought enthused
excitement ought to pay his member's fee;
we all have been accusing and accused
of notgettingititudinosity.

But though we may agree or disagree—
and all the world is out there to be cruised—
a constant flow of good-will is the key
to properly disposing of our used
notgettingititudinosity.

Rocky Dilemma

We all have prejudiced associations
that, hard as we may try, we can't control—
a vocal cue will prompt improper relations
we'd like to bury in a psychic hole;
we bite our tongues, avoiding confrontations,
and bit by bit we learn the proper role,
and out of all our inner storm and stress
we chose what to express—and not express.

Natasha Trethewey has now become
the poet laureate—and no Celt more than I
is with her now within the seething scrum
of Yankee English, nor more approves her high
award, nor more aware of the sometime hum
that subjugated languages supply
in assonance, inflection, or in rhythm—
depending on the tones surviving with them.

But those are not the accents that I hear
when someone says the poet laureate's name—
and those are not the accents that will sear
my writhing inner self with childish shame;
what accent comes most clearly to my ear
with foreign vowels I desperately disclaim
in prejudice that I cannot deny?
Natasha saying "Moose and squirrel must die!"

AIR GUITAR

Bit by bit they deconstruct the thing:
no frets, no pegs, no bridge, removing its
harmonic parts until at last each string
is slack, and lacking resonating bits.
They put the rest, the body, neck, and head,
aside as too much like a prop for those
whose earnestness is all they need instead
of craft and art to fake that they can sing.
So there they are, on either stage or page:
the foremost poets of the modern age,
who, writing their relineated prose,
will swagger as they grimace, strut, and pose
pretending they are better than they are
while playing nothing but an air guitar.

Ode at a Poetry Reading

My head aches as some frowzy mum explains
    In psychiatric detail how her drugs
Have freed her and yet kept her in her chains,
    And after every poem gamely plugs
Her book. I sort of envy her her lot
    As, all too sober, I remain aware
        I have no fashionable brain disease,
        And think no odious thought
Except my lack of sympathy for her despair
    Among such colleagues victimized as these.

Give me a draft of verse that makes it seem
    They've read more than a medicine bottle label,
And has more than a narcissistic dream
    To be about—but I don't think they're able.
Give me a stanza full of the need Keats
    Or Shelley had to write a brilliant line,
        Or Byron's wit, for poetry is hope
        And not free verse deceits
Whose artlessness pretends that all is fine
    Descending down this well-intentioned slope.

They ought to read. And then read more. Find out
    What those up at the lectern haven't known,
A fret and fever passionate about
    The way clay, motion, hands, and will have thrown
A well-wrought urn, instead of some unshaped
    Unpolished mud that's only set apart,
        The moderns and postmodernists exclaim,
        Because it has escaped
The question whether it is really art
    By anyone who happens to sign their name.

Let's get away from here or else I'll hurt
    Somebody's feelings—or else let's find a drink
So if I have to listen to this blurt
    At least perhaps I'll manage not to think
Too meanly while they tenderize the night
    By bludgeoning it with language as they whine
       That poverty is bad, injustice worse,
         And might does not make right,
As if they were the first to ever divine
    That power won't like truth in prose or verse.

The stage is bright enough that I can't see
    The glass in front of me, but ah! I smell
The piquant liquor cooling in the scree
    Of ice cubes clicking softly. Now the swell
Of voices starts to murmur where it blared
    To my annoyance only a swallow ago
       And fade as sip by sip the still-warm night
         Blurs by, and I've declared
One swallow may not a summer make, still though
    The first one can make everything all right.

Darkly I listen, and sometimes now and then
    I note with half an ear some phrase's breath
That wanders over close to meter again
    Then sighs, and dies its leaden prose's death;
Now, more than ever, alcohol seems rich
    In promise as they pour out from their pain
       Their endless woes, a flowing golden shower
         Over the mic by which
They amplify their voices and, in vain,
    Attempt to amplify poetic power.

Free verse was born as prose, and prose it stays;
    No hungry generations make it more.
These voices here this passing night don't raise
    The bar at all among the free verse corps.
It's just the same old therapy for free
    That AA offers all who will confess
        Their powerlessness over their addiction—
            The same except that we
All wave the magic charm that makes our mess
    Seem less our own by claiming that it's fiction.

Fiction! Ah, the word is like a spell
    That we can use to write of witch or elf
Or spouse or child or boss or what the hell
    We please, pretending that it's not our self.
But now the host announces how he's pleased
    With such a turnout, and asks we tell our friends
        The reading schedule—the depth to which he's sunk—
            And so we're gently eased
Outside, our memories fleeting as it ends,
    Or is that only me—who's slightly drunk?

THE SEAGULL

for Liam Guilar

Eating lunch beside Lake Erie, reading literary theory,
Continental jokers who'd innumerately misconstrued
   Philosophy, I heard a flapping, a riffled book or sandwich wrapping?
And suddenly a whoosh like clapping snatched my sandwich as I chewed;
Not relatively, absolutely, snatched it!—if you'd been there you'd
     Have seen the gull that stole my food.

There, the first day of September, a day I always will remember,
There went dark the last faint ember dying warmth had disembued
   Of any hint of heat or fire: Fish, de Man, the whole entire
Continental crew, their pyre dead and cold. Which, I conclude,
Resulted from empiric action, that is what I must conclude,
     By the gull that stole my food.

There is no silken, sad, uncertain rustle of some final curtain
Sweeping by across the stage to close a bad play unreviewed;
   Instead there is a seagull standing, out of reach as others, landing,
All demand, are each demanding, something for each seagull brood—
Eyeing me and each demanding something for its seagull brood,
     Behind the one that stole my food.

I took my strength from their sheer number: let the Continentals slumber,
Slumber as we unencumber Western culture to exclude
   The willfulness of the obtuse that hides behind confused abstruse
Enjargoned terms that introduce no clarity to theory skewed
By incomplete misapprehension of the pseudo-math they spewed,
     Refuted by my stolen food.

Then that seagull still beguiling all my fancy into smiling,
Smiling as I, now reviling all postmodern thought, pursued
    Whole schools of relativistic thought through briary fields of is and ought;
Who fled as if by whips pursued, postmoderns realizing who'd
Become the newly naked nude, the newly-naked sometime-nude,
        Exposed by gulls who stole my food.

This I sat engaged in guessing, but no syllable expressing
To the gulls whose greedy eyes no Derrida could so delude
    As he'd deluded half a culture; that pseudo-philosophic vulture
Stood revealed: a culture vulture soon to hear his thinking booed—
Or would except the sneaky bastard died before he could be booed—
        Booed because of stolen food!

Then, it seemed, the air grew denser, acting as a gull- dispenser:
Flocking gulls flew flapping flying fleetly through the murk accrued.
    "You!" I shouted, "don't deprive me of the proof I need to drive me.
Do not say you're here to jive me, jive me so that I'd conclude
Conclusions that I might conclude, conclusions that I must conclude!"
        Said the gull "Whatever, dude."

"What's the point of such a sortie to the real in flocks of forty?
Are you representing Rorty, conversation's foulest mood?
    How I hate that spieling spielist—yet, you stole my lunch, the realest
Thing that's happened to intrude into my consciousness, a rude
But rousing rudeness that renewed empiricism stealing food!"
        Said the gull, "Whatever, dude."

"Sophist! I would like to punch you in the beak! You ate my lunch,
You stand there like there's still a bunch you'd say if you were interviewed
    About the philosophic fictions fighting the unjust depictions
Possible amid the flows philosophers have always spewed,
Amid the turgid purging prose philosophers have always spewed!"
        Said the gull, "Whatever, dude."

"Sophist!" said I, "On the level tell me whether you still revel
In postmodernism's devil-spawned and -raised non-pulchritude!
    Tell me what it's all about: can empiricism flout
Postmodernists' pernicious doubt with realism's stolen food?
Will beauty, justice, good, proportion, finally be again pursued?"
        Said the gull, "Whatever, dude."

"Be that word our sign of parting, bird or fiend!" I shouted, starting—
"Back you go into that tempest warlock, witch, or devil brewed!
    Leave no white plume as a token of that lie your soul has spoken!
Leave my loneliness unbroken!—all my loneliness accrued!
Take your beak from out my heart, depose my form from off your rood!"
        Said the gull, "Whatever, dude."

Now the seagull, never flitting, still is sitting, still is sitting,
Out of reach but within spitting distance, posed with attitude.
    And his eyes have all the beady dead indifference of the greedy
Since I shot and stuffed him as a symbol of that interlude
Of doubt between attractive options, a doubt that ought to be pursued—
        Unless you say "Whatever, dude."

Modern Cybernetizen's Song

Netizen:
I am the very model of a modern cybernetizen
All logic I dispense with, and all taste and manners jettison;
I come in every stripe—from the conservative to radical,
And know it all accept for how to spel, or write grammatical.
I haven't got a clue about the use of logicality
And drivel on with made-up-factoid bargain-bin banality.
I'm found on TV, radio, and many other medias,
But cyberspace is where I'm most particularly tedious.

> Geek Chorus:
> He's found on TV, radio, and many other medias,
> But cyberspace is where he's most particularly tedious.
> Yes, cyberspace is where he's most particularly tedious.

Netizen:
I flame opponents hairless from a dozen different pseudonyms
Each one a ruder, lewder pun on Anglo-Saxon crudonyms—
And where I find civility and hot debate have been at ease
I break it up with spamming, flaming, scrolling, and obscenities.

> Geek Chorus:
> And where he finds civility and hot debate have been at ease
> He breaks it up with spamming, flaming, scrolling, and obscenities.

Netizen:

I'm known for disputatiousness and other sorts of knavery
From purposeful mendacity to things yet more unsavory.
I'm ignorant in every field, poetic to statistical,
Which only makes my points of view more thoroughly sophistical;
My attitude's aggressive, and my tone is sanctimonious,
My facts are bad, conclusions wrong, and arguments erroneous.
My posts are pure unparagraphed expressions of my vanity
Impossible to parse except perhaps for the profanity.

> Geek Chorus:
> His posts are pure unparagraphed expressions of his vanity
> Impossible to parse except perhaps for the profanity!
> Impossible to parse except perhaps for the profanity!

Netizen:

In short when I can tell you why I'm such a dull vulgarian,
And why my selfish egocentric views are libertarian,
And why my sense of humor roots about in prepubescency
As if I don't quite understand the cause of my tumescency,
Or why my only mode with love is jokery and jestering
While fear of being hurt leaves all my real emotions festering,
You'll know why I'm at home alone abusing my puerility,
Compulsively exhibiting my manual facility.

> Geek Chorus:
> You'll know why he's alone at home abusing his puerility,
> Compulsively exhibiting his manual facility!

Netizen:

Wherever civil reason is accounted most iniquitous
You'll find me absolutely inescapably ubiquitous.
In short, all logic I reject, all taste and manners jettison,
Because I am the model of a modern cybernetizen!

> Geek Chorus:
> In short, all logic we reject, all taste and manners jettison,
> Because we too are models of the modern cybernetizen!

MUSING ON THE BOSS ART

About suffering they were never wrong,
The old managers: how well they understood
Its harrowing power; how they took pride
In placing blame directly where it does not belong;
How, when those pursuing excellence are waiting
For the miraculous raise, there always must be
Perky-breasted new hires who survive by skating
On excuses at the edge of a not very good
Performance rating.
But even the most dreadful tongue-lashing must end
In a corner office, or the hall outside,
As the prairie-dogging cube-dwellers turn away,
And under-managers pretend they cannot see,
All relieved that the disaster did not spray
Its harsh, forsaken splash on them, and they pretend
There's no important failure. Fluorescents drone
As they had on the white face disappearing into the down
Elevator, and the expensive suits, whose every frown
Is feared, disperse, each trailing a delicate scent of cologne.

HAMLET'S NEIGHBOR'S SOLILOQUY

To yell, or not to yell—that is the question:
Whether 'tis nobler, in the house, to suffer
The bikes and footprints of outrageous children
Running across my lawn, or scream my troubles
And, by opposing, shoo them. To vent, to rant—
No, more: and by a rant to say we end
The gouges, and the thousand natural shocks
That lawns are heir to. 'Tis a cultivation
Devoutly to be wished. To vent, to rant—
To rant—perchance to scream: ay, there's the rub:
For after rants parental calls may come
That we have frightened from our fertile soil
The neighbors' kids who gave us cause. Respect!
I'll bear the calumny my whole long life.
For who would bear the tire tracks of kids,
The knee-holed grass's green now compromised,
The pangs of despised feet, the law's delay,
The insolence of parents, and the spurns
That patient weeding of the unworthy takes,
When he himself might make his voice be heard
Through an open window? Who would footprints bear,
To grunt and sweat behind a weary mower,
But that the satisfaction of scaring off
To undiscovered countries of other lawns
And wish them no return, fires the will,
And makes us rather chase these kids away
Than hope their hopeless parents punish them?

Thus the suburbs make old geezers of us all,
And thus the native hue of toleration
Is goaded into action past restraint,
And the pale cast of thought is thrust aside
With disregard for children gone awry
And lose the name of neighbor.—Soft you now,
Here comes a bunch—I slide the window up:
You kids! Get off my lawn!

THE FEET

Retail salesmen on their feet,
    Painful feet;
Oh what a world of anguish comes from reinforced concrete.
    How they bitch and moan and squabble
        In the break room in the back
    Though no grunt nor groan nor sob'll
    Pass their lips as off they hobble,
As you see them straighten, striding to attack,
    With their smiles smiles smiles
    As they walk their weary miles
Through a million I'm just looking's from the customers they greet
    On their feet, feet, feet, feet, feet, feet, feet,
On their archless, bunioned, corned, and callused feet.

See the salesmen on their feet—
    Well-shod feet—
With orthotics, gels, and cushions, some that cool and some that heat.
    See the salesmen as they're feigning
        That their pain will go away;
    Watch the smile that's slowly waning
    As the customer's explaining
That the item is just perfect but it can't be bought today.
    Oh how silently they curse
    As the client packs her purse
And repeats that she'll be back because the salesman's been so sweet
    On their feet, feet, feet, feet, feet, feet, feet,
Their eleven-hour work-day aching feet.

Then they walk with lagging feet
    Laggard feet:
The manager has called them to his comfortable retreat
    Where they'll find that he is docking
        Them, the thing all salesmen dread,

When delivery went knocking
    They had found the client balking
At the timing or condition or they've changed their minds instead;
    And the manager is yelling
    At such goddamned over-selling
And to get it back together or be put out on the street
    On their feet, feet, feet, feet, feet, feet, feet,
On their over-promising under-performing feet.

Once at home they soak their feet
    Swollen feet
Then put them on the hassock while they find the strength to eat
    From the meal they bought while sitting
        In the drive-thru in their car—
    And they do not mind admitting
    That they know it isn't fitting
But they just can't stand to stand; another stride's a stride too far;
    They don't even walk upstairs
    They just fall asleep in chairs
While they dream they've got a job where they are working from a seat
    Not their feet, feet, feet, feet, feet, feet, feet,
Not their not-yet-rested unrecovered feet.

They will not admit defeat
    About their feet;
They massage and wash and shoe them whether plus-size or petite.
    As they limp about preparing
        For another working day
    With their rheumatism flaring
    You can hear them softly swearing
While they get their heads around another entry to the fray.
    When they get out on the floor
    You can't even tell they're sore
They're so friendly, smiling, chatting, reassuring, and discreet
    On their feet, feet, feet, feet, feet, feet, feet,
    On their you would never know it hurts them feet.

MINOR DEITY

for Kathleen Ossip

I sing the minor deity
of not quite drunken gaiety
whose altar stands where time and place combine to seem just right;
where clergy and the laity
can speak with spontaneity
And sly half-lit salaciousness seems witticism's height;

When seated in a dinery,
the atmospherics winery,
as everyone enjoys each moment's magical delight,
the conversation's finery
is nuanced, never binary,
and no one who was there forgets that long enchanted night;

One may espouse astrology,
one's favorite theology,
or claim events evolve without a goddess, dark or light—
whatever ideology
there's much more to cosmology
than zealous self-promotions that pretend the truth is trite.

So do not cling so stodgily
to what you hold is modually
unsympathetic sneering when opponents say black's white.
Our voices may be codgerly
but sing, if somewhat dodgily,
the praise of minor deities if only just for spite.

GANDHI

The loincloth Gandhi wore to greet
　　　　His followers was small—
While super-callused soles showed feet
　　　　That wore no shoes at all.

His fragile health reduced his meals
　　　　Until he looked like death—
The journal of his wife reveals
　　　　His halitosis breath.

He followed odd and mystic ways
　　　　Down paths to strange effects—
So mystic that his wife got praise
　　　　But never any sex.

He changed the world through fatalistic
　　　　Will and sheer osmosis—
This supercallusedfragilemystic-
　　　　hexedbyhalitosis.

Modern Lit

I taught a class on modern lit. We read
poems, novels, stories, and tales from all
around the world, from places the students said
they hadn't known existed—except for Paul.
The Great Leap Forward, and Mao, were news to them;
Rwandan genocide was entirely new;
apartheid they learned they should condemn,
but only after Paul gave them a clue.
All semester, over and again,
Paul knew the well-known facts of peace and war—
the facts the others should have known by when
they got to class, and mostly well before.

One morning when I mentioned Cecil Rhodes
someone wondered who he was, although
she could have googled him—such skill erodes
on purpose if there's someone who might know
for just the asking—but I only smiled
and said one thing that Rhodes had done was name
a country for himself. They seemed beguiled
one man had ever had such power and fame.

Then as I said "Of course they do not call
it 'Rhodesia' any more, it's called ..." I blocked
completely on the modern name. And Paul,
who saw at once my memory was locked,
slowly said "Zimbabwe". At his "Zim-"
it flooded back, and '-babwe' we said together.
I shook my head and sadly looked at him.
"I had forgotten." He shrugged as if whether
I had or hadn't didn't matter. "Well, you,"
I said, "are an American who is head
and shoulders above the rest." He blushed and threw
His hands up. "I'm Canadian," he said.

Tazer

Madison and West One Hundredth Street
used to be a bank branch office. Now
Olympic Guns and Ammo gives discreet
service there. I'd been wondering how
to find an extra-special something sweet
to show Herself that I'd been thinking "Wow!
That's just the thing!" in order to amaze her,
and so I bought a battery-powered Tazer.

If you are not familiar with this tool,
a 9-volt battery gives a low-amp shock:
you simply stick the prongs into the fool
who's messing with you, push the button, and rock
his world till he falls twitching in his drool—
while you, before the twitching drooling stops,
sashay away and leave him for the cops.

At home, I put a battery in and pressed
the button. Nothing! Man, what a rip!
A nasty arc was what I'd hoped. I guessed
this model didn't have the proper tip.
I looked around for something I could test
this brand-new toy on, so I snapped a zip
at that threatening refrigerator door—
that made a mark I'll get in trouble for.

But there I am alone with this new toy
and 'Just one 9-volt battery?' I thought;
'That can't be all you need for some bad boy
who's coming at you.' I haven't fought a lot,
but I know you don't want to just annoy
the guy, you need to give him quite a shot.
I picked up the directions. For reading those
I perched my reading glasses on my nose.

But first, I thought, I'm going to get a beer
and sit back in the La-Z-Boy to read.
A burst one second long, it says right here,
disorients assailants, and two would lead
to muscle spasms, and three would mean severe
loss of control, and make the guy proceed
to flip-flop like a lying politician,
and leave him moaning in the fetal position.

And all the time I'm looking at this thing,
no bigger than a pack of cigarettes,
and thinking there's no way this thing can bring
assailants to their knees in quivering sweats
whenever they might try to take a swing,
and let you walk away with no regrets.
On a single 9-volt battery, they say—
I sat there reading thinking 'There's no way.'

So, drinking in my t-shirt and my shorts,
directions left hand, Tazer in my right,
deciding that I don't trust these reports
and ought to test this thing before a fight
will find it leaves some guy just out of sorts
instead of putting out his goddamned light,
and there was Trixie, 90 pounds of trust,
looking at my beer with canine lust.

If I was going to give this as a gift
designed to be the acme of protection
I had to know it wouldn't give short shrift.
I eyed the dog with no small circumspection
and thought a couple seconds is pretty swift
and dogs don't have that good a recollection.
Trixie looked at me without a doubt.
I knew I had to try this thingie out.

I touched the prongs against my naked thigh
and pushed the button. If you ever feel
you want to try a Tazer out, well, I
would like to caution you about the real
exposure time, for things will go awry
at once. There's no 'one-second burst' to deal
with, first of all, because you can't let go
until it's knocked away by some greater blow.

What seemed to happen to me was Seal Team Six
appeared and picked me up and body-slammed
me over and over while beating me with sticks.
I woke up feeling like the hung-over damned,
wondering how I got into this fix,
my nipples burning, and my left arm jammed
painfully through the recliner's inner workings—
trying to control my twitchings and jerkings.

It took a while but I sat up to take
a little stock of who and where I was.
My left leg was a bit inclined to shake,
my right side had a tendency to buzz.
I'm pretty sure that I was still awake
because it hurt all over, as it does
when you have found out once again that you
have failed to think another thing quite through.

I was in the kitchen on the floor,
the recliner in the other room on its side,
my reading glasses broken by the door.
I wasn't really hurt, except my pride,
and cleaning up was going to be a chore.
A good thing I was there at home alone
cause everything smelled like a piano-bar microphone.

And then I heard it. Trixie was making a whine
and gurgle sound that I had never heard.
I felt that sick panic, stomach and spine,
and said more than one unprintable word
as I staggered up. But she was fine, just fine:
She'd only got to lick the last, deferred,
small sip from the beer bottle until today—
today was a puddle, and she was lapping away.

Washing The Car

The day turned nice; I thought I'd wash the car.
But walking down the hall I saw the trash
was full and, taking that, I check the plant
that's drooping next to the glass of iced tea
that I'd forgotten, by my Ray-Ban sunglasses,
and wait, isn't that the bedroom remote?

Okay, so first I'm going to take the remote
right back upstairs. And so I set my car
keys down on the hall table beside my sunglasses
and carry the remote and the can of trash
toward the stairs—but I could use the tea
before I go, couldn't I, to water the plant?

No, the last time I watered a plant
with something not water I got that remote
treatment from Herself. I leave the tea.
I glance out the window at the car
as I trudge up the stairs with the trash.
It is getting sunny. I'll need my sunglasses.

So making a mental note to pick up my sunglasses,
while I'm by the desk upstairs, I plant
myself in the chair to pay the bill for trash
collection but, before I do, I put the remote
into my pocket, and wonder where the car
keys are, and think "Oh, downstairs by the tea."

And so I head back downstairs toward the tea
with the trash, trying to remember my sunglasses
and then get on outside to wash the car.
But first I have to water that drooping plant.
I turn to go to the kitchen and knock the remote
inside my pocket against the can of trash.

The TV goes on upstairs. I set down the trash
and, reaching into my pocket, knock over the tea
with my elbow as I'm trying to work the remote.
In the kitchen, I calmly find my sunglasses
in my hand, get towels, water for the plant,
and go clean up, muttering about the car.

So now the trash is still full, my sunglasses
are back beside the tea, by the watered plant;
and chances are remote I'll wash the car.

QUARRY

The sun was green and hazy in the trees
and in the clearings it was getting hot.
Though I was not quite lost enough to sweat
still, duff on duff, a map across my knees,
lost enough to check if what I'd brought
would take me where I thought I had to get.

The old maps couldn't tell me where to go
except in a sort of vague and general way.
The roads and towns on modern maps had changed,
and hills and streams were all that I could know
were pretty close. But even those that day
appeared to have been gently re-arranged.

Or else the maps were wrong. I'd finally found
the spring way west of where it should have been,
beside it, often-fixed, the smashed-up still.
Making escape is always dangerous ground:
the ways are opened, hidden, and opened again,
and maps mis-marked to hide a hidden hill.

But then, I didn't really have in mind
a clear idea of what I'd hoped to find—
except that maybe using maps so old
showed places now forgotten with the way,
and all but legends dead, so I could say
I'd made my own way through what I'd been told.

TRAIL

The branches blacken and the colors pale
amid the steady stutter of the rain.
The mist has dampened sunrise to a glow.
This muddy way cannot be called a trail—
cold, wet and dirty, last year's leaves remain
to almost hide the little signs I know.

Halfway down a gulley I hear the creek
that quickly trickles past and down the hill,
and see the landmark log I'm looking for.
A silent rip of mist gives me a peek
at what's ahead: my track continuing still
up into woods, but then it's mist once more—
except I thought I saw up on the rise
a sudden turn I didn't recognize.

LEANING

I'm leaning toward a trip to Tennessee,
to lean against a fence, and watch the sky,
and smell the dusky coming-on of night:
that scent of cooling-down and work-day done.
I'll watch the sun retreating up a high
and rounded hill of blues and greens that turned
to reds and golds failing in the fading sun.
I'll feel the urgent stretch that every tree
will make uphill to catch the sunlight's last
bright shine, as if the highest hilltop burned
with flaming leaves that beckoned up to me.

I'll lean as if I walk against the grade,
to stretch uphill myself, my shoulders past
my feet, inclined to try and stay upright
on any cant. I wish that I were there
already, leaning on my slanting pitch
to keep me climbing upright toward that bright,
brief beacon, struggling up the hill
where everything must lean into the true;
I wish that I were up there on that height,
and stretching up and leaning toward that light
to catch a little bit of that final shine,
to claim that something beautiful is mine
before the cold and dark take hold tonight.

51 Poems

Acknowledgements

Back on the Tour
Rotary Dial, March 2015

Broken Sunlight
Antiphon, Autumn 2013

Dancing With Abandon
Rotary Dial, November 2014

Dark Fails
Rotary Dial, March 2015

Feet, The
Rotary Dial, February 2015

Giving Up For Lent
Yggdrasil, June 2015

Hamlet's Neighbor's Soliloquy
Bluestem Magazine, December 2015

Have You Forgotten
forthcoming from 826

I Like You The Best
Quarterly Review, December 2014

Leaning
Rotary Dial, October 2015

Me and the Moon
Snakeskin, January 2015

Musing on the Boss Art
Salt River Review, January 2001
Poemeleon, Winter 2006

Ode at a Poetry Reading
Rotary Dial, March 2015

Old Fighter Pilot
Rotary Dial, February 2015

Poet Bios
Rotary Dial, March 2015

Poetry Reading
Crisis Chronicles, December 2015

Racquetball
Rotary Dial, April 2015

Seagull, The
Rotary Dial, March 2015

Tracks
Rotary Dial, June 2015

Trail
Rotary Dial, October 2015

Ubi Sunt
Rotary Dial, October 2015

World Remakes Itself, The
Rotary Dial, October 2015

16445252R00056

Printed in Great Britain
by Amazon